Puppy Love Colouring Book

Morgan Fitzsimons

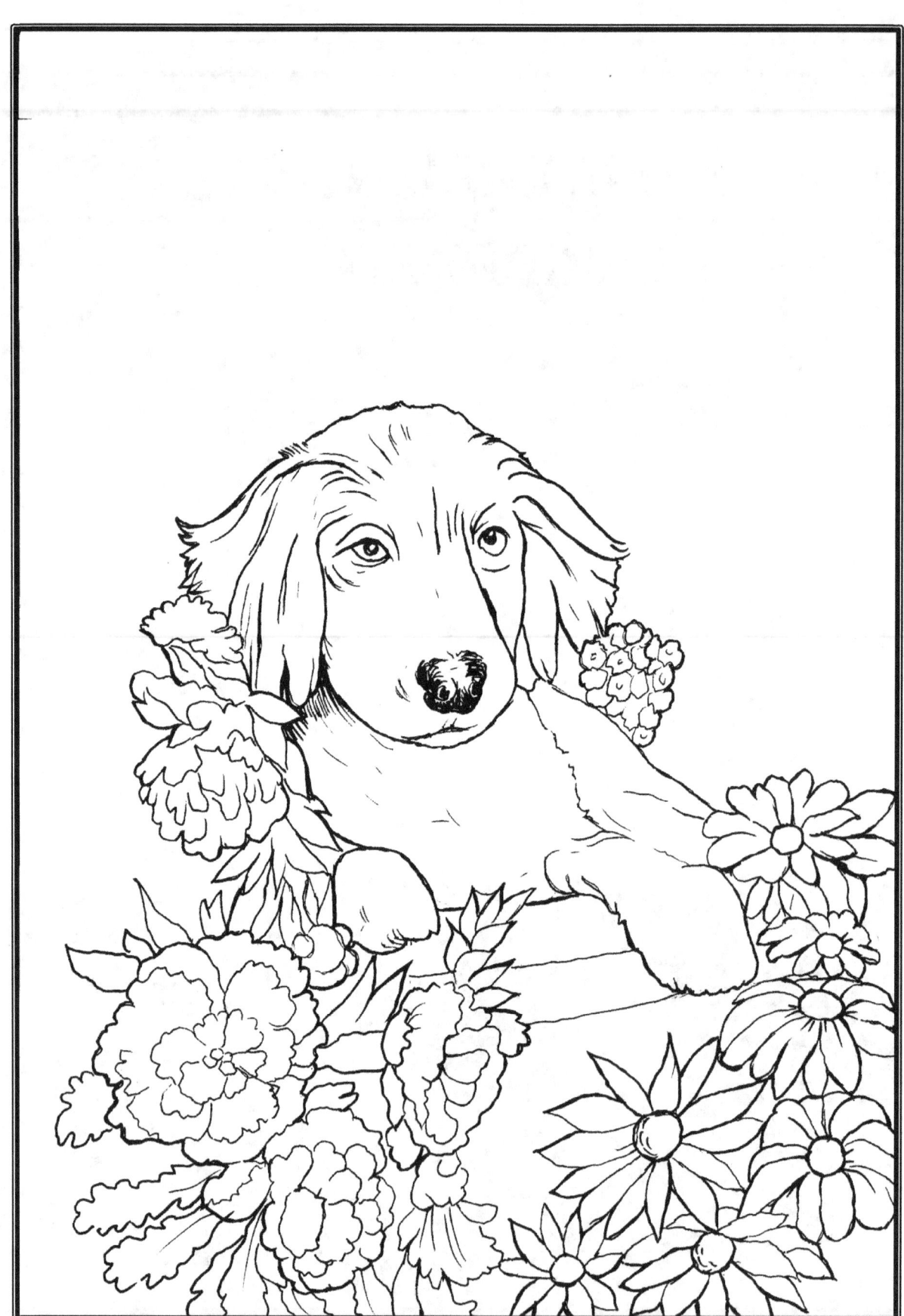

Puppy Love Colouring Book

Artwork By
Morgan Fitzsimons Author-Artist

Graphics Layout By
Linda Larson

© *2017 Morgan Fitzsimons*
All Rights Reserved

No part of this book may be reproduced, stored in a retrieval system, or transmitted by any means without written permission of the author.

Published by Fae Entertainment & Fae Workshop

ISBN #978-1-7750241-6-3

Published and Printed in All Countries Worldwide

Printed in Paperback

info@Fae-Entertainment.ca

www.MorganFitzsimons.com

www.FaeEntertainment.com

www.Fae-Entertainment.ca

www.ArtStampsStore.com

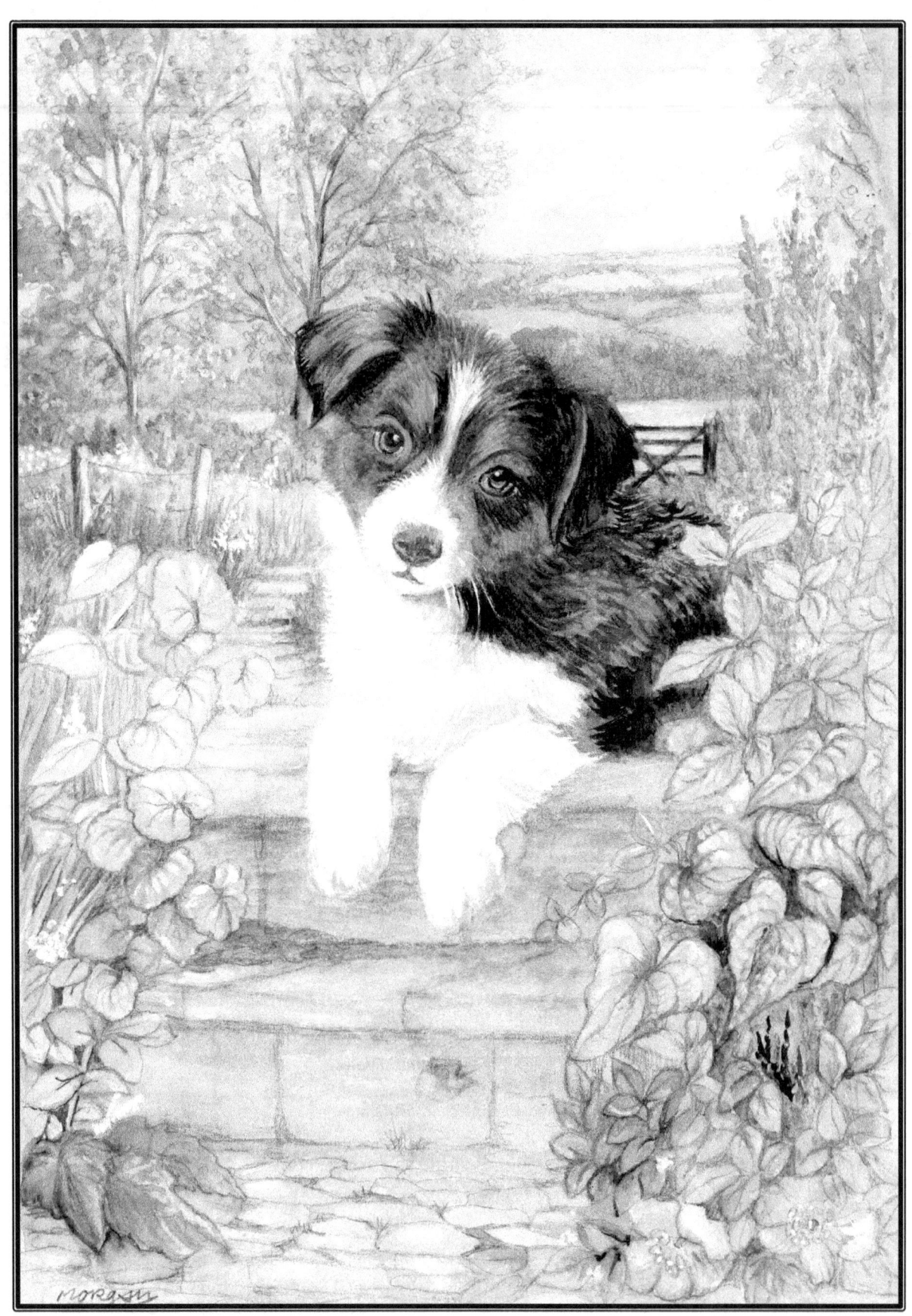

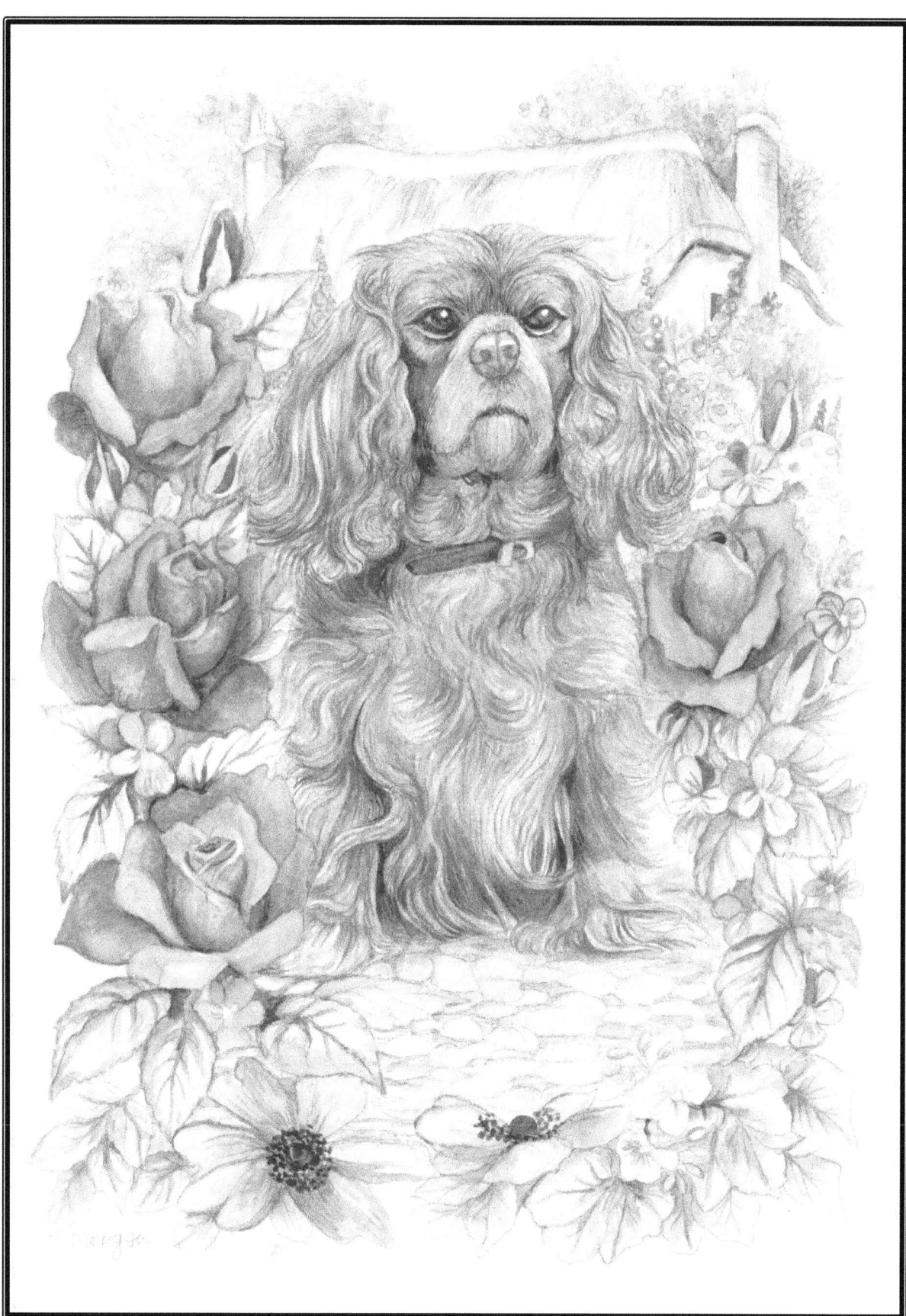

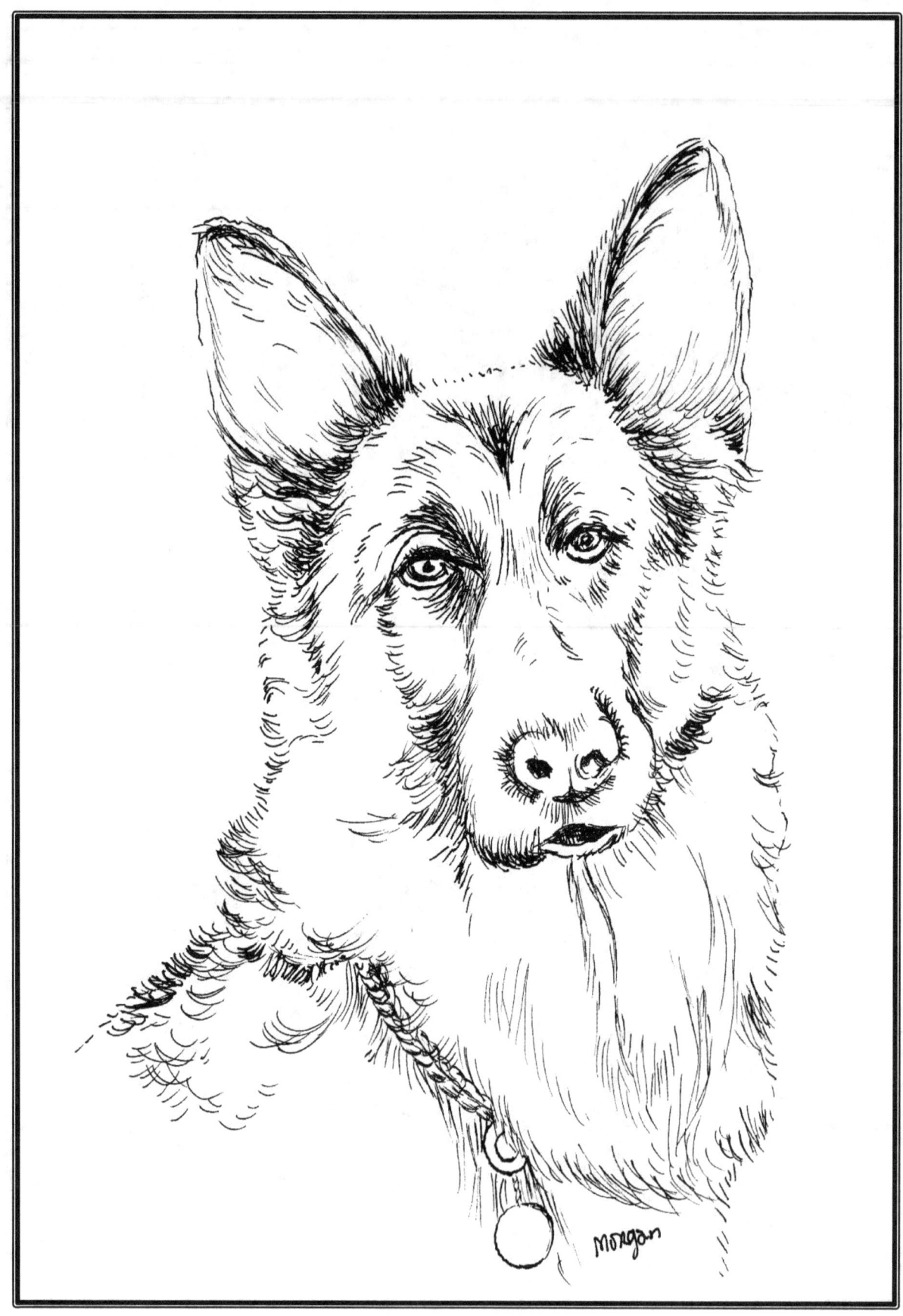

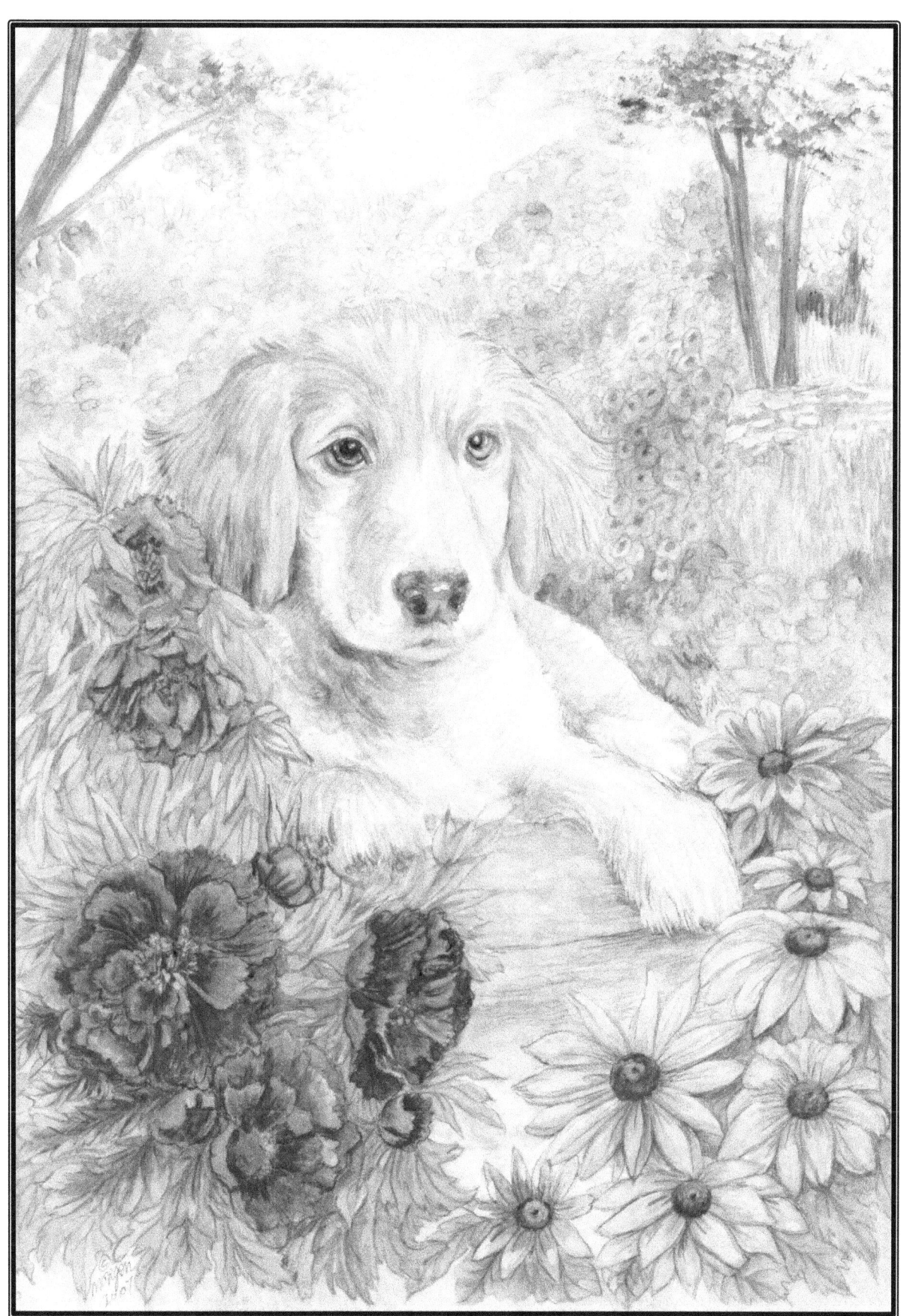

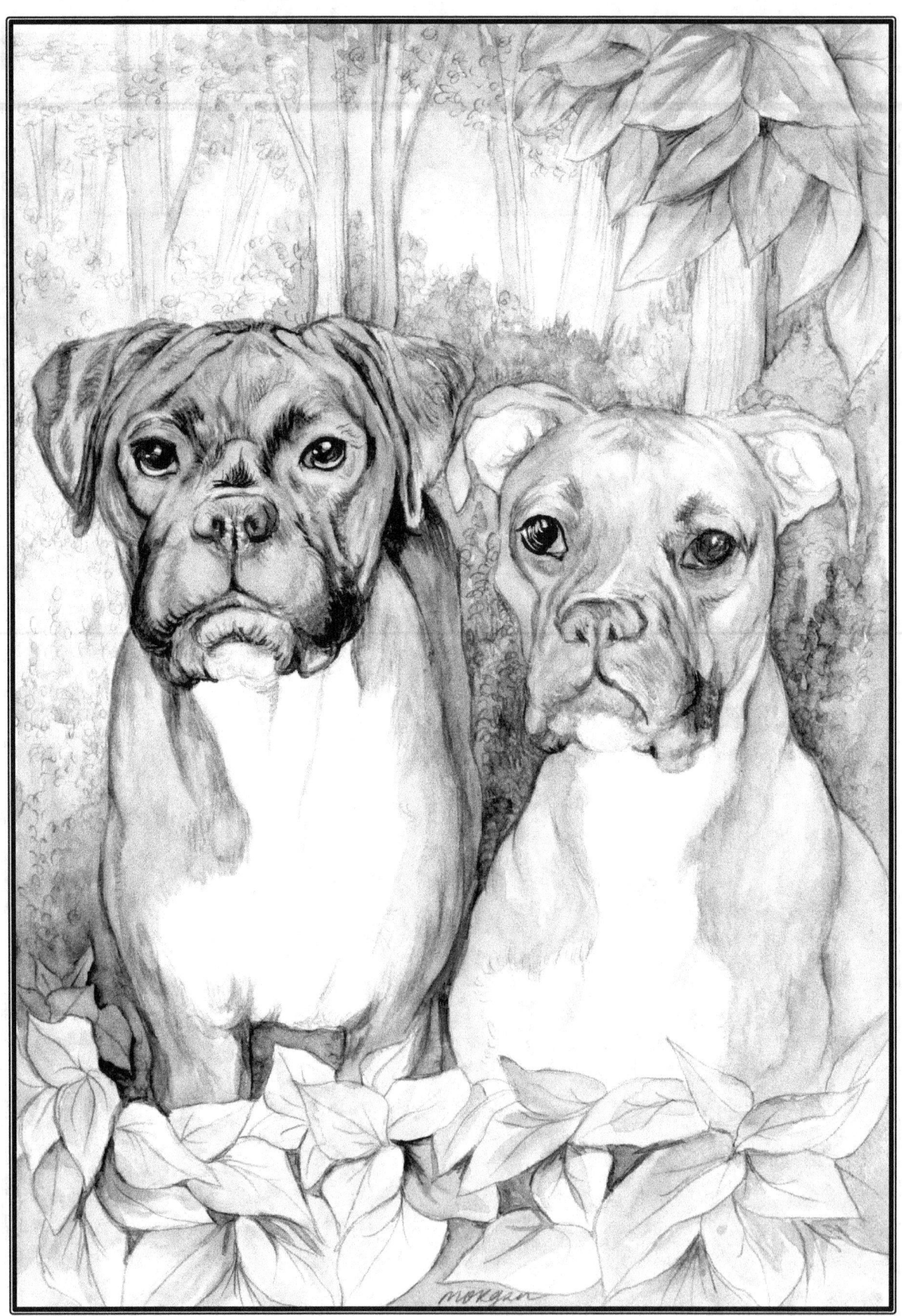

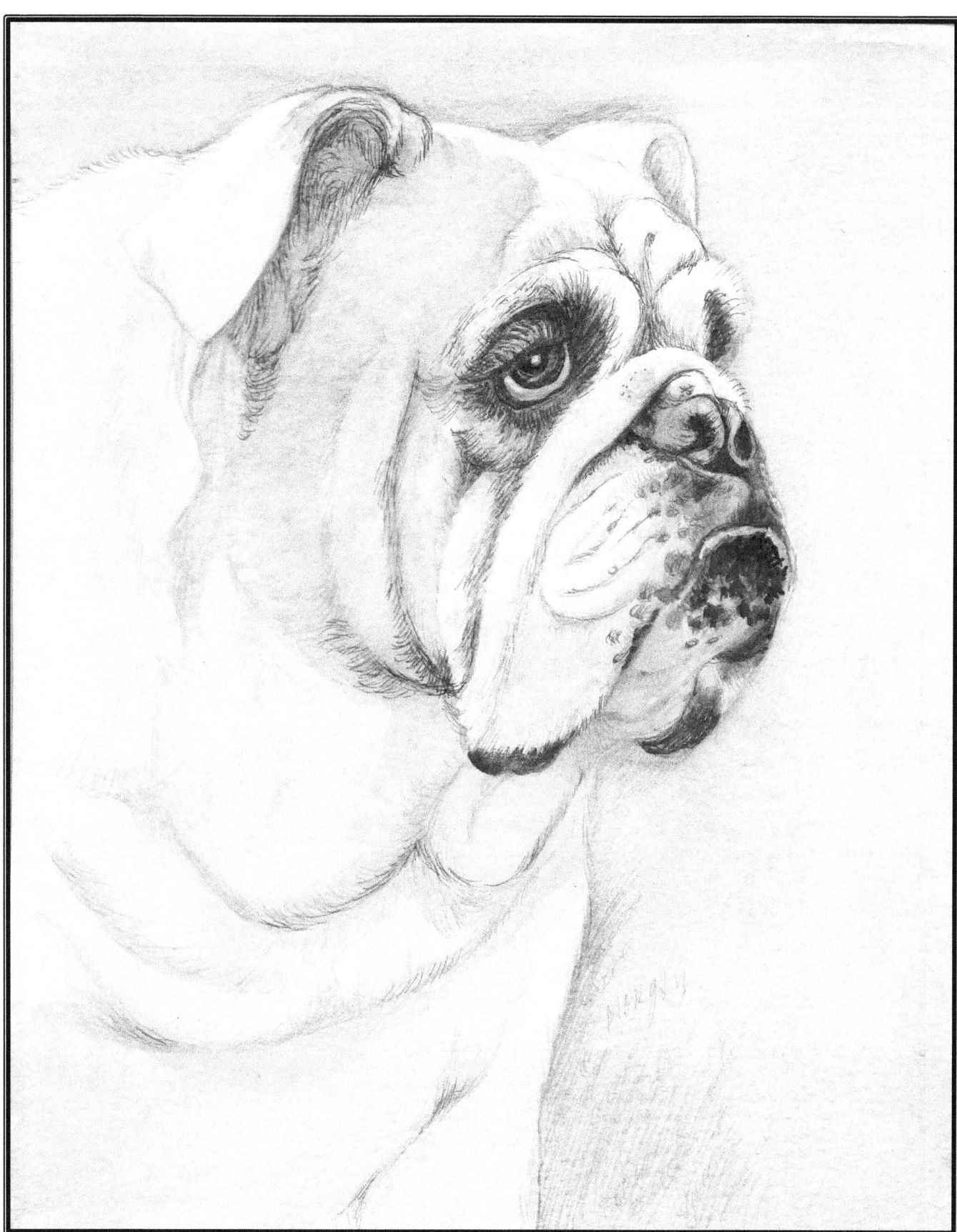

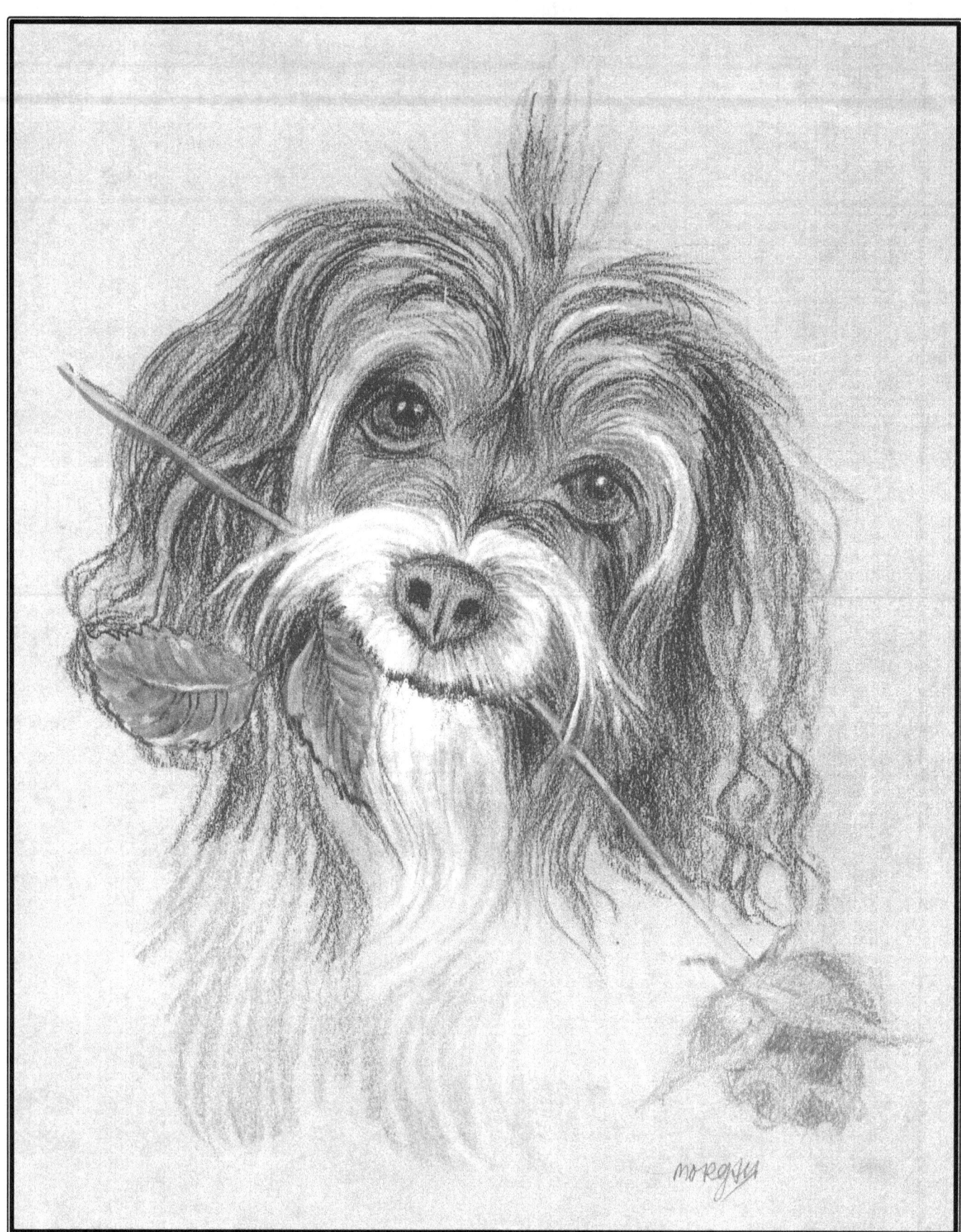

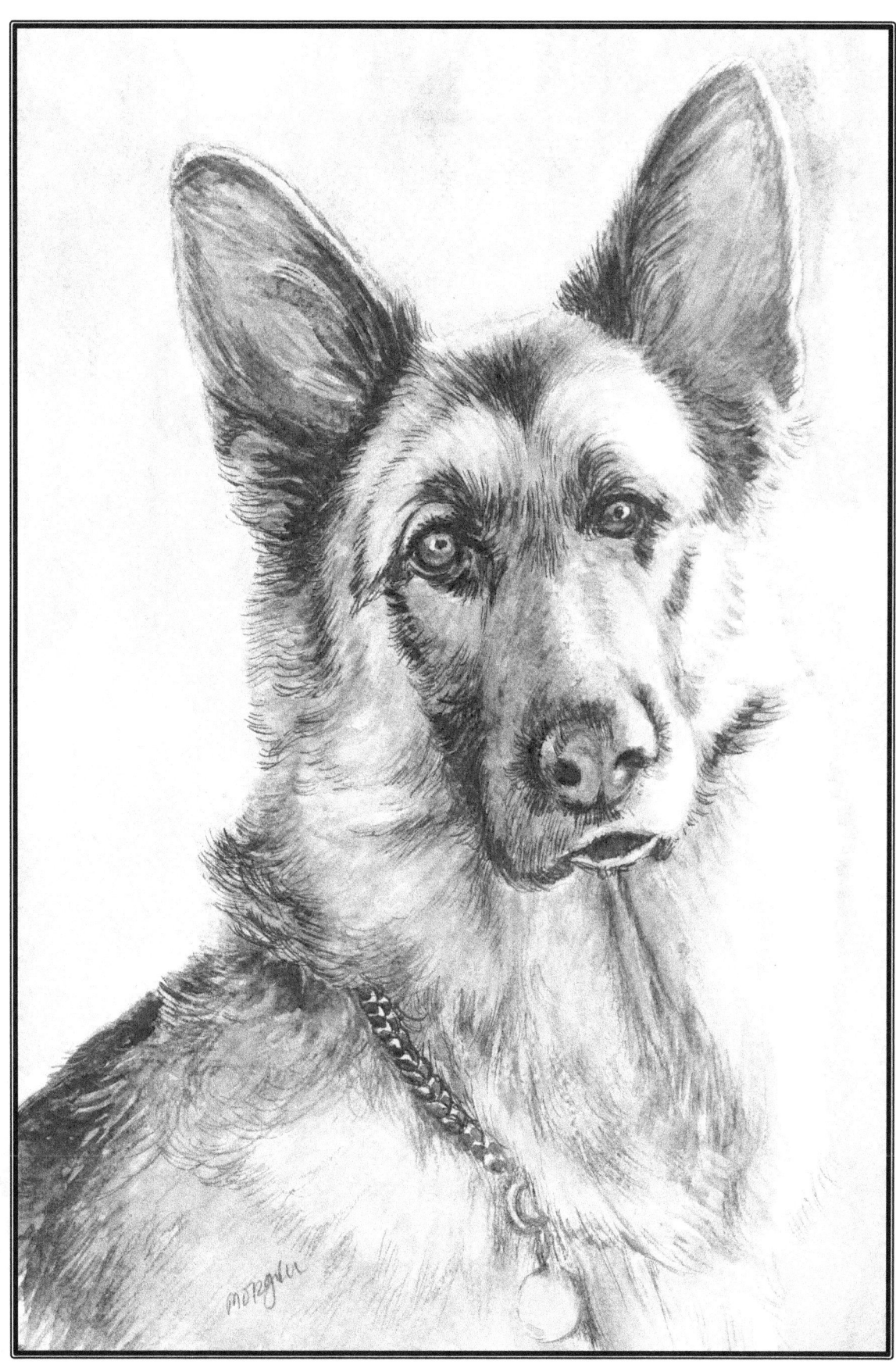

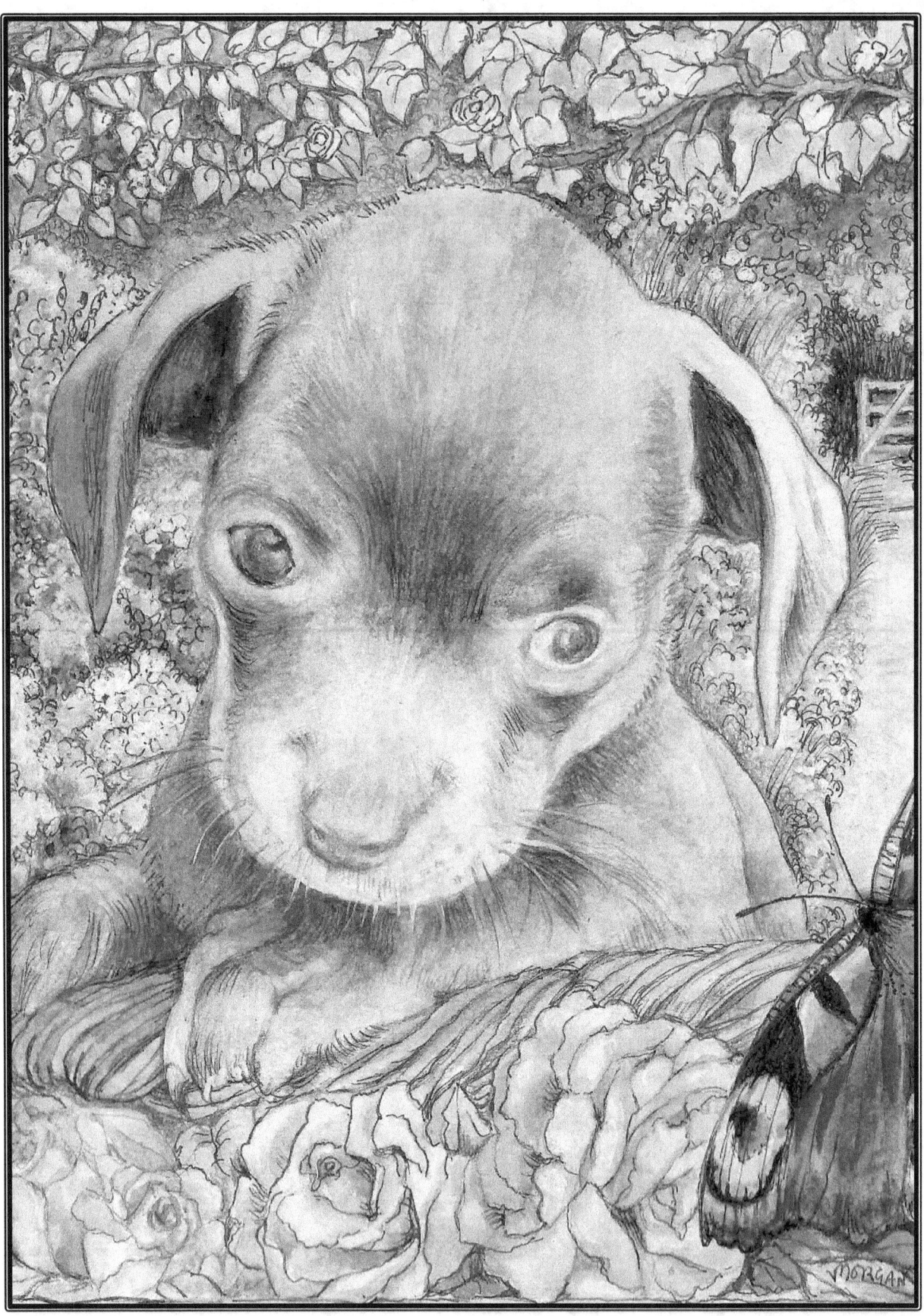

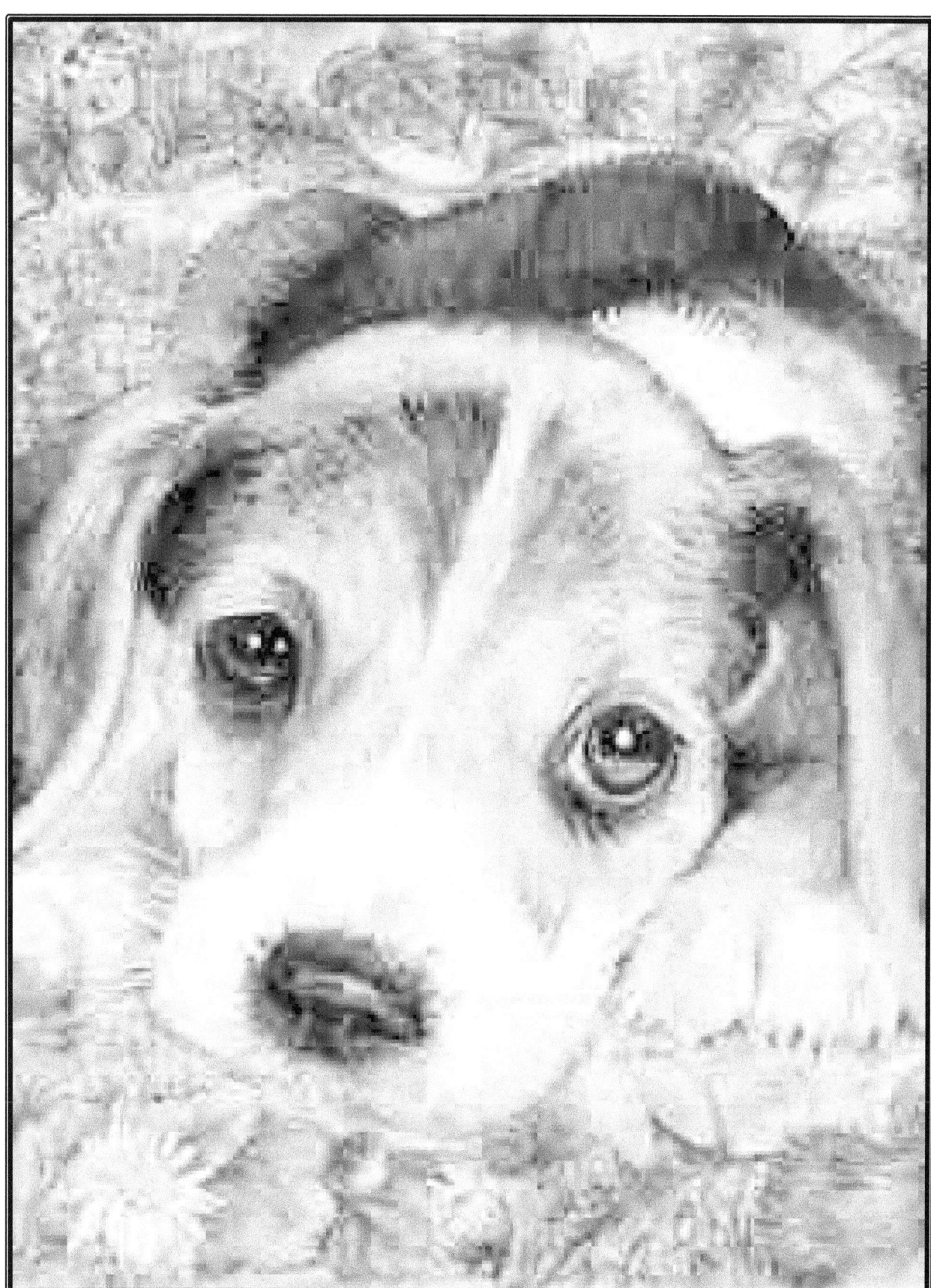

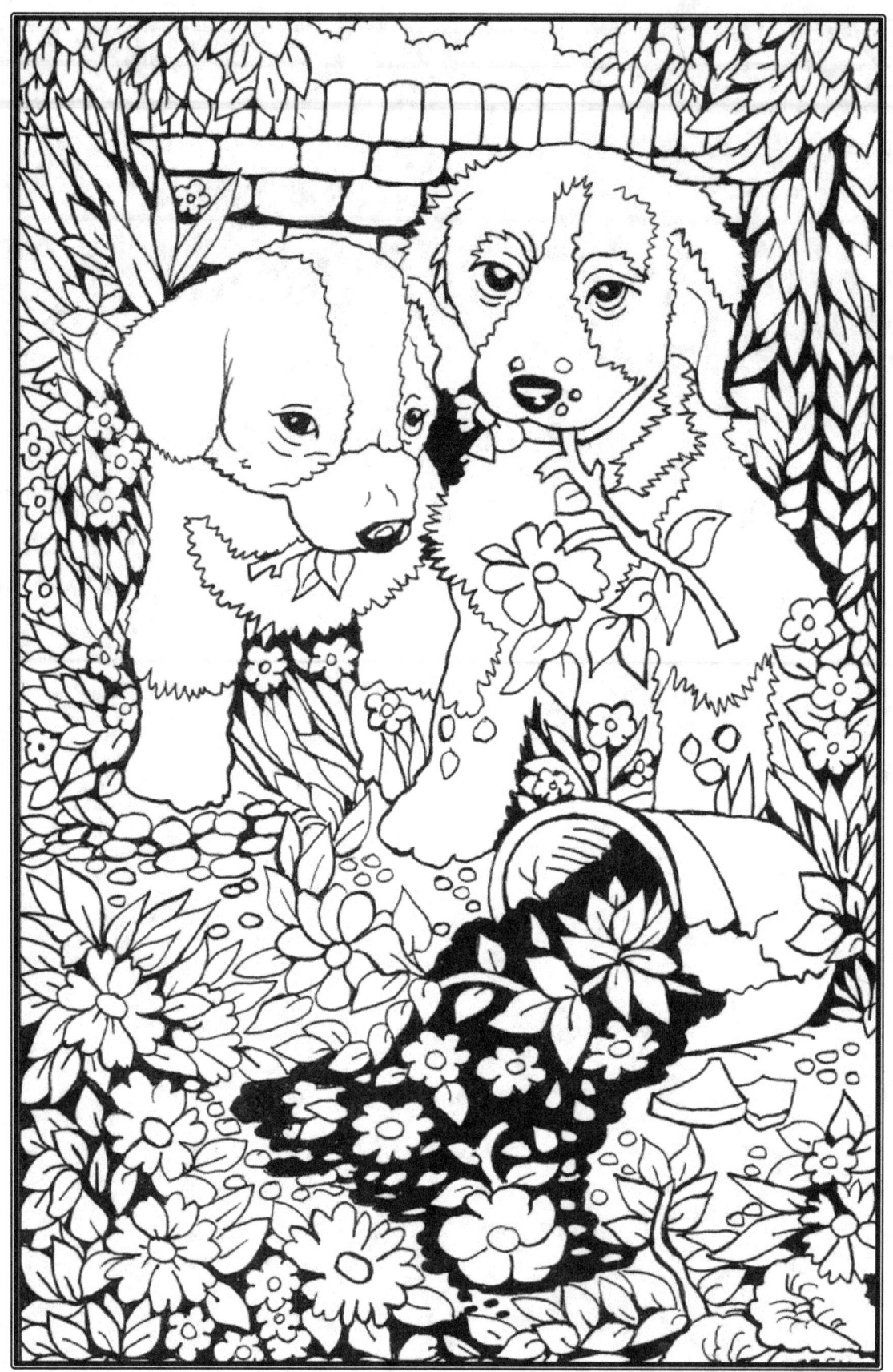

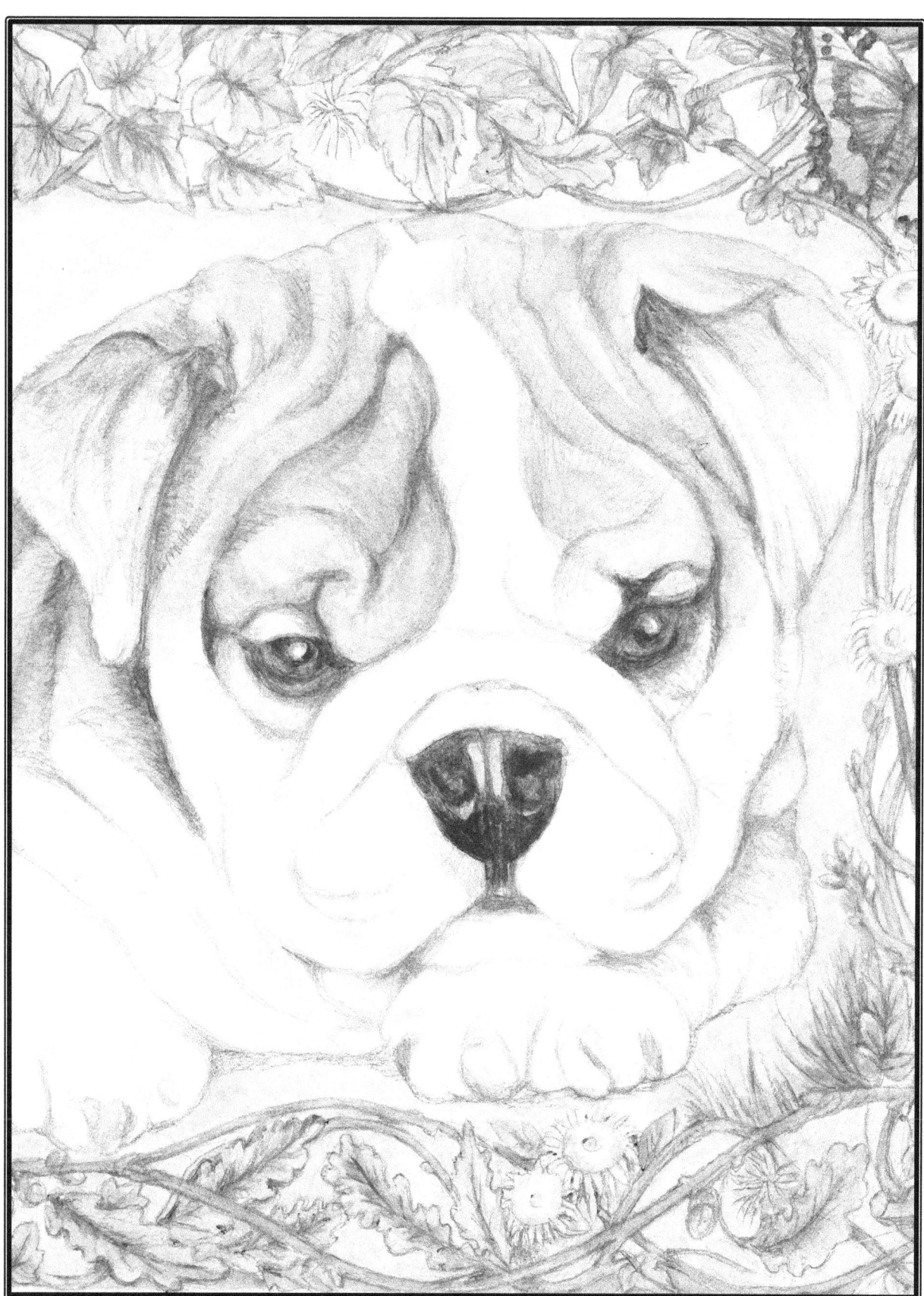

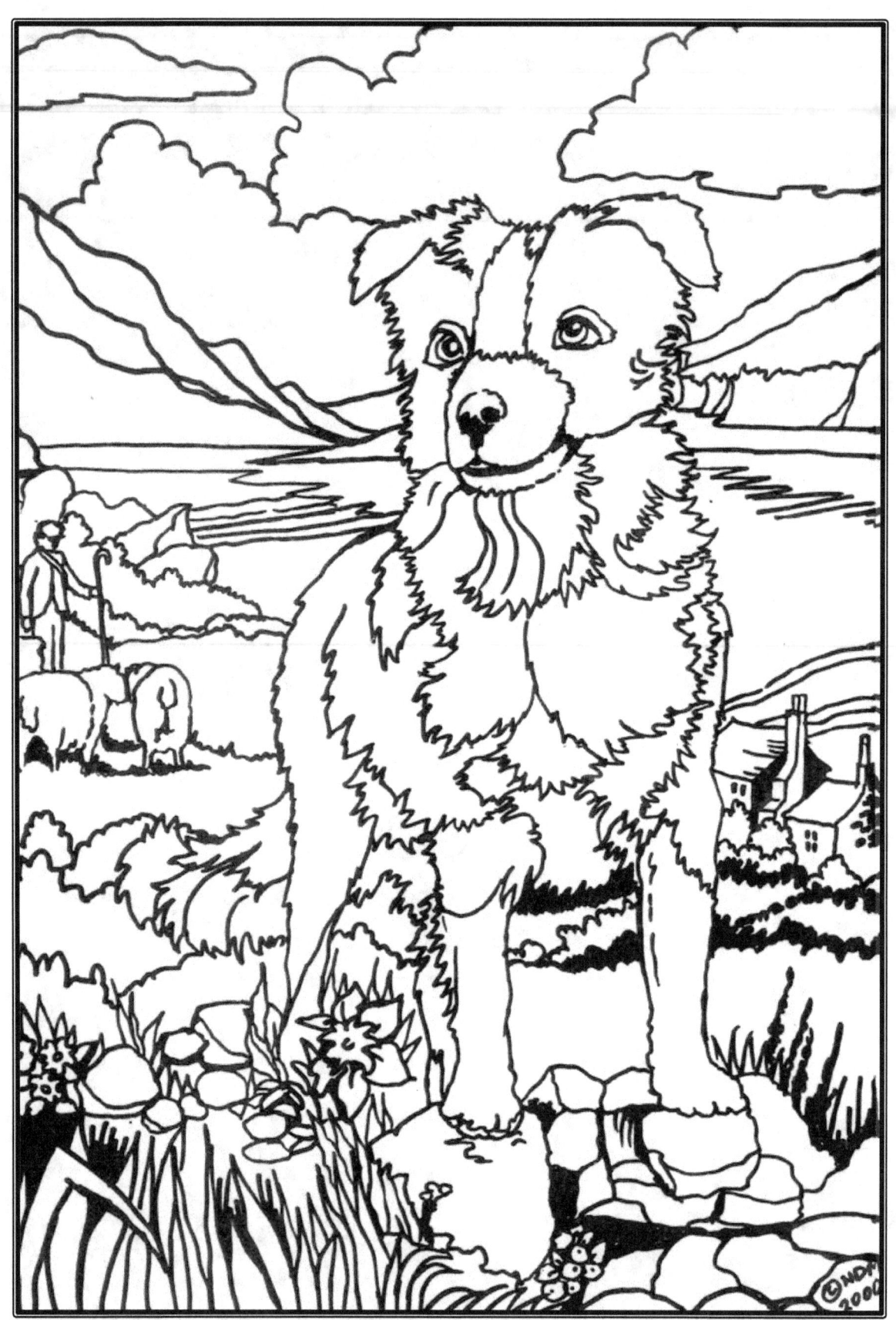

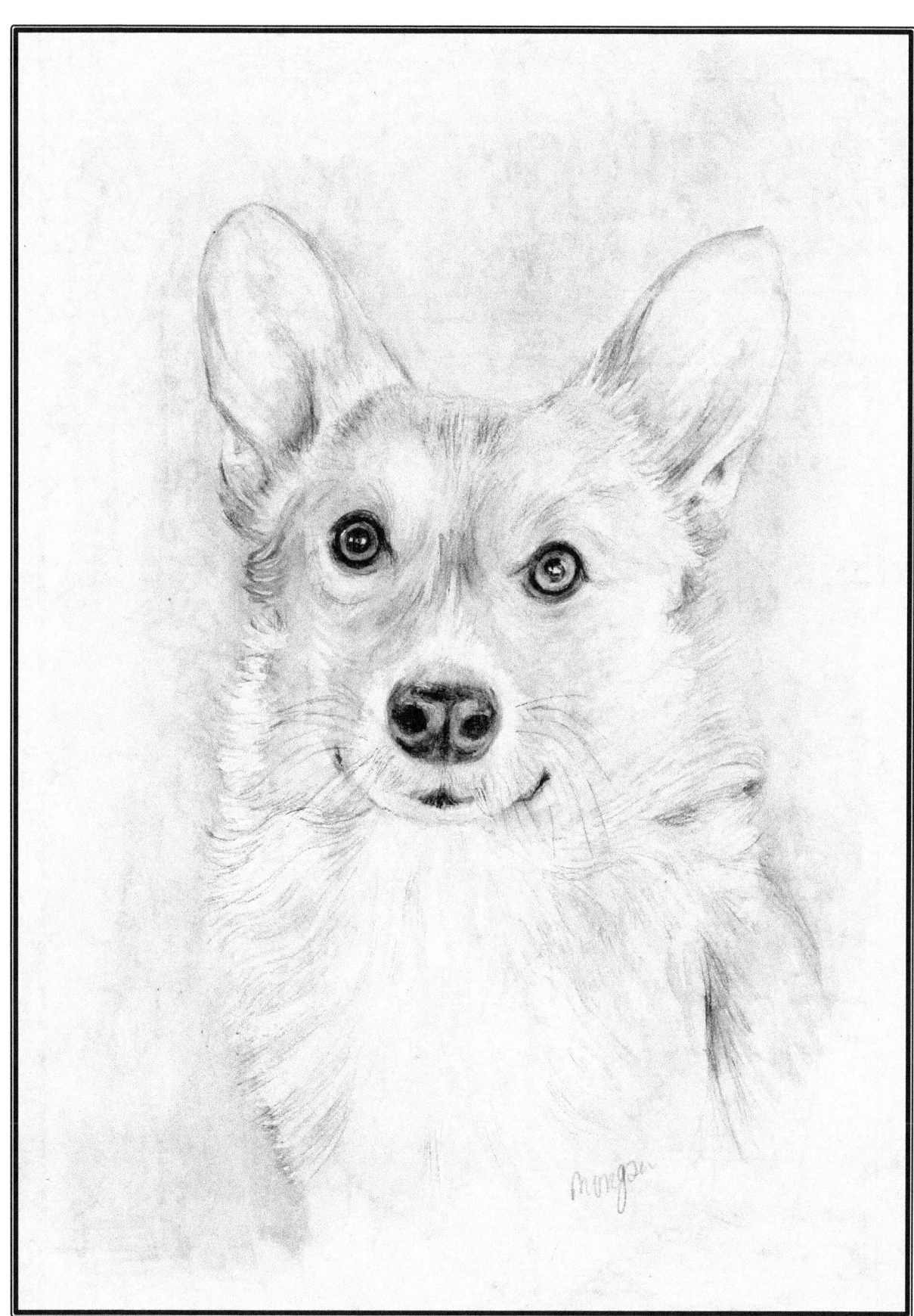

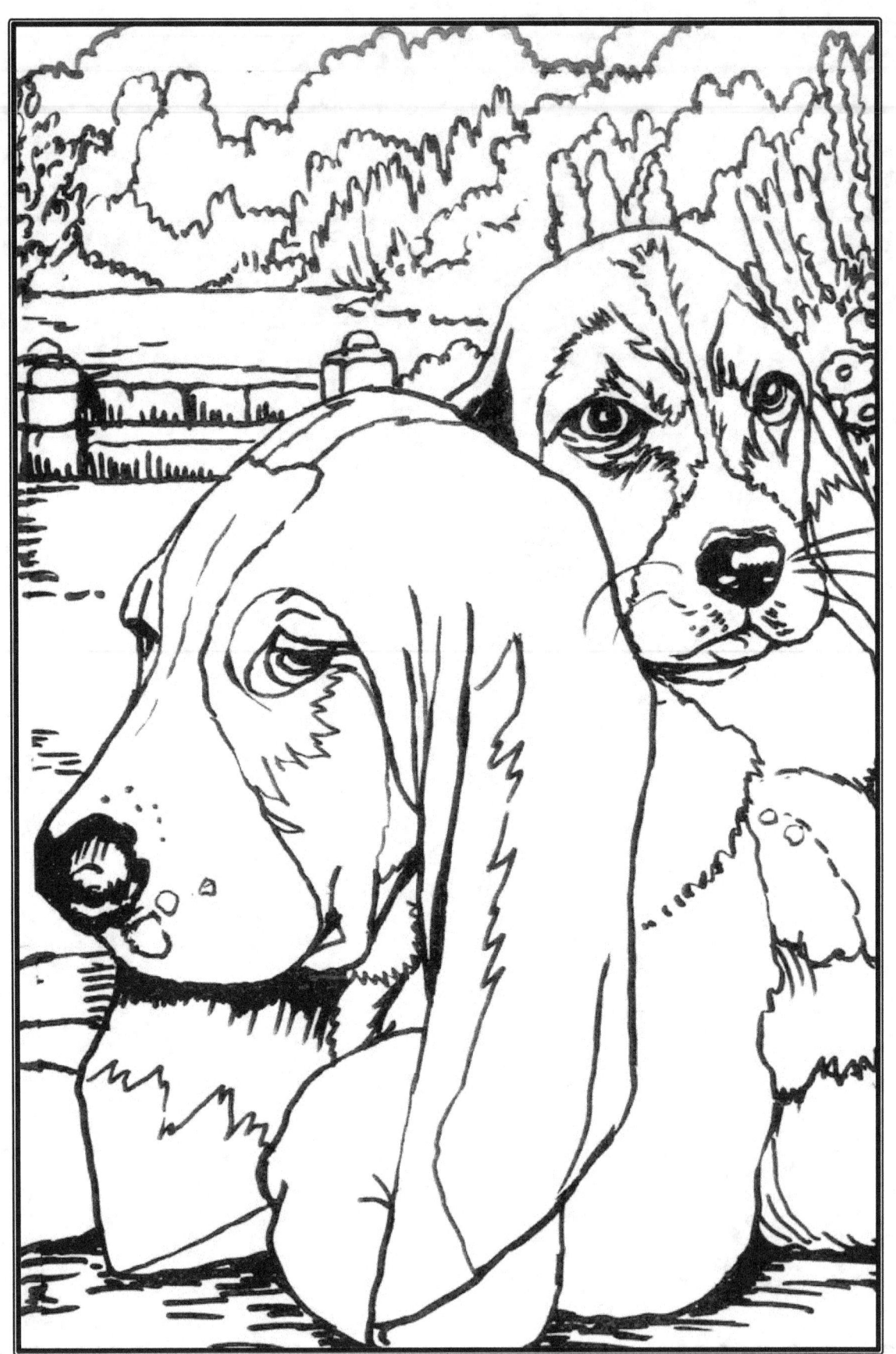

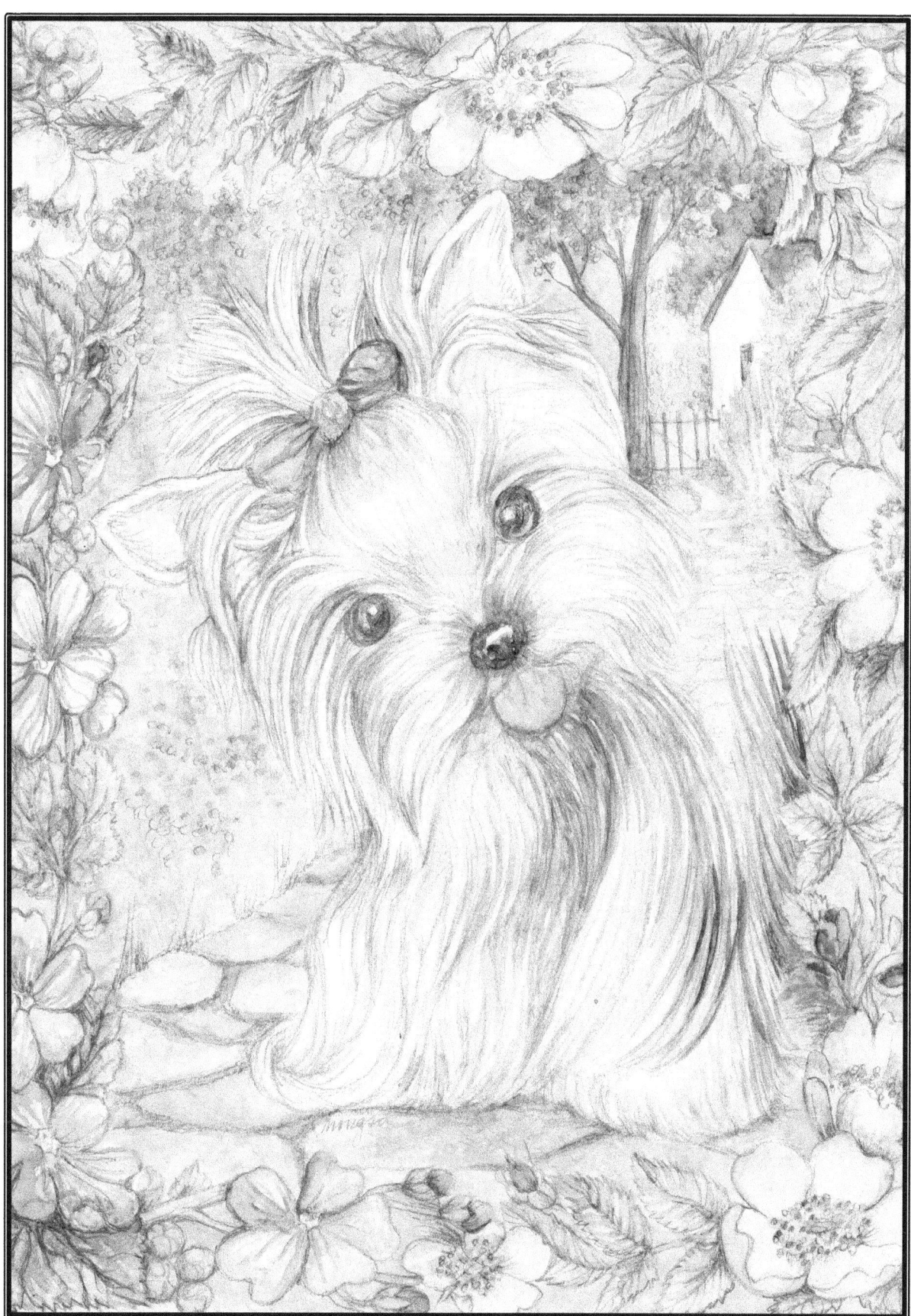

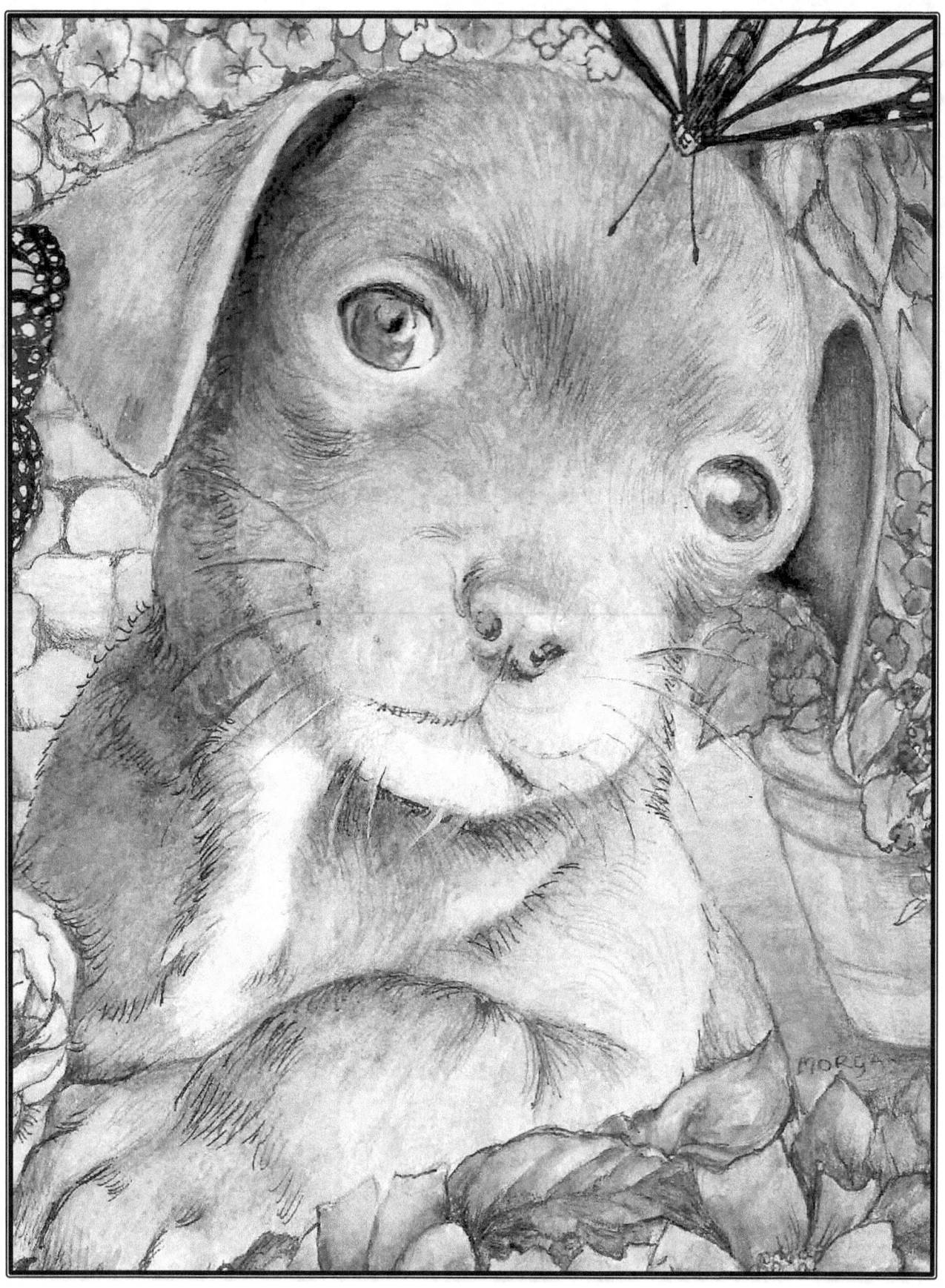

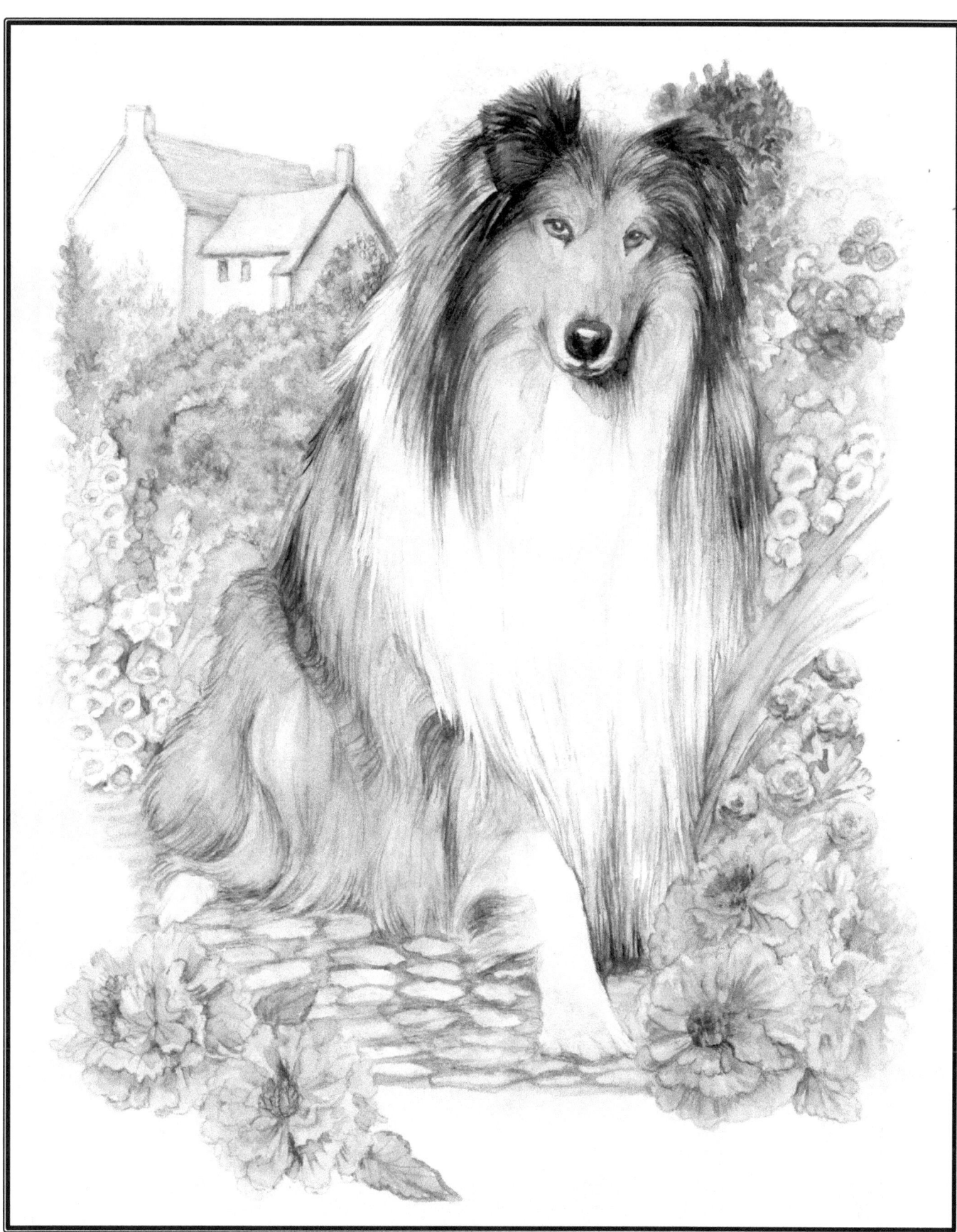

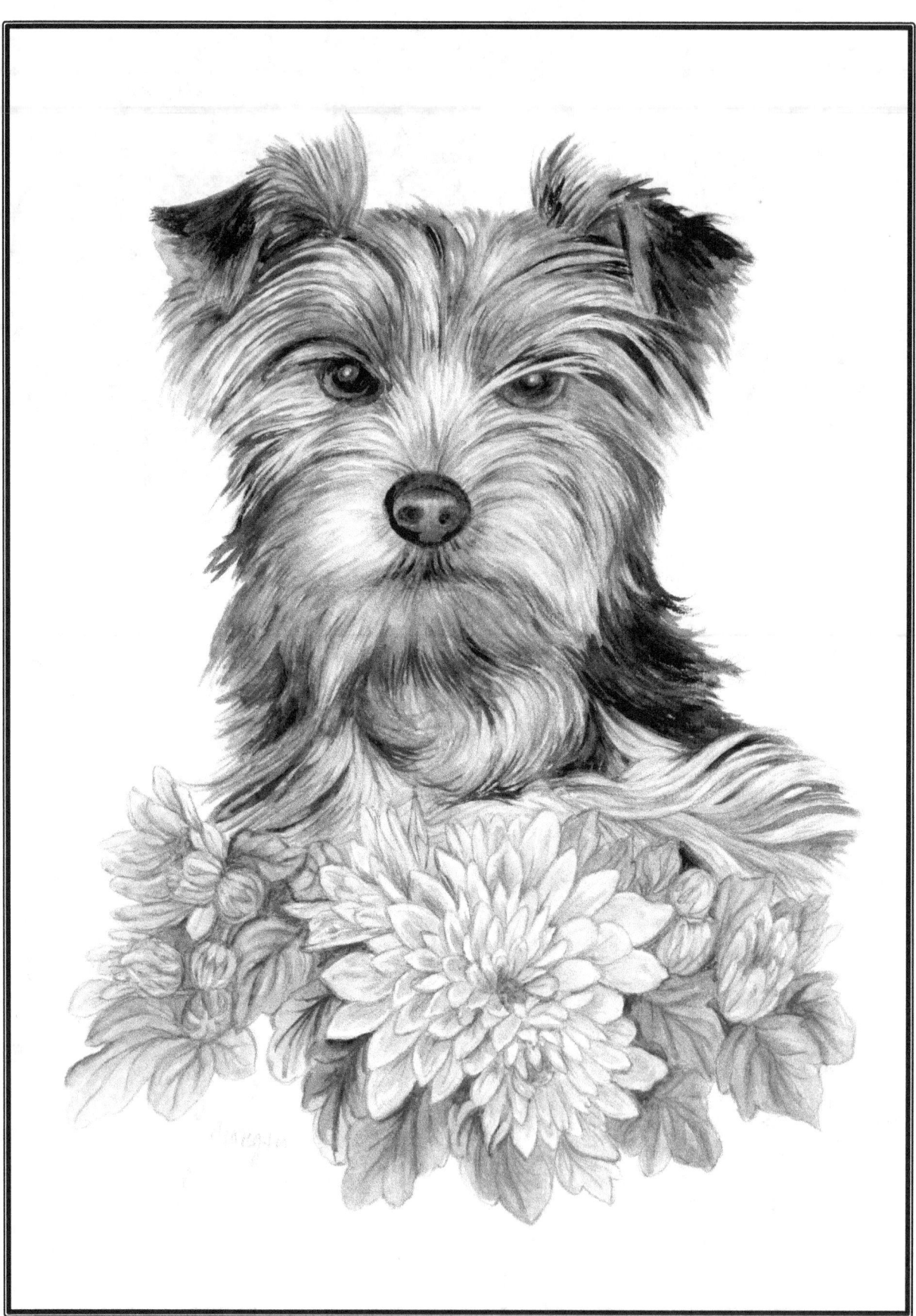

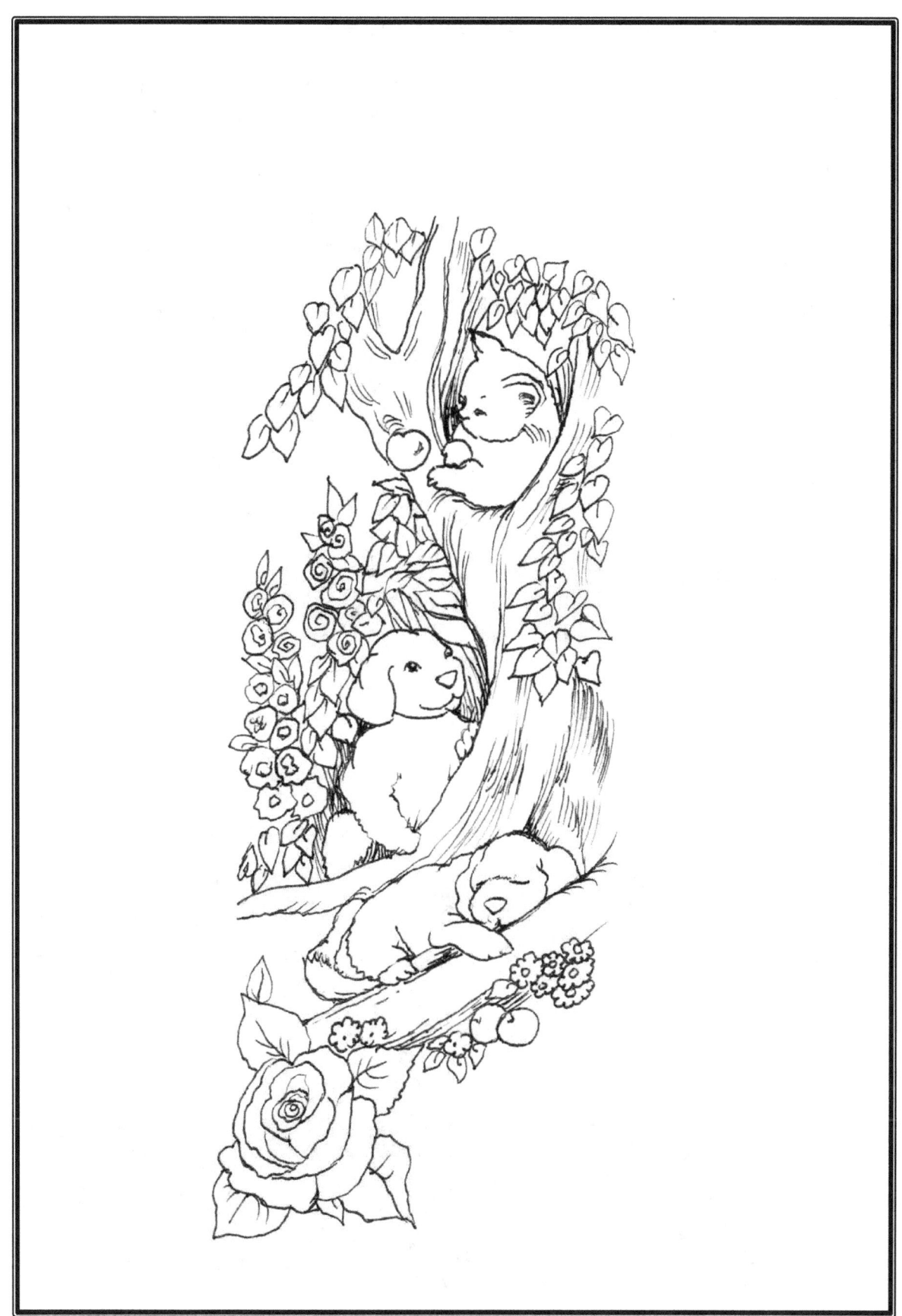

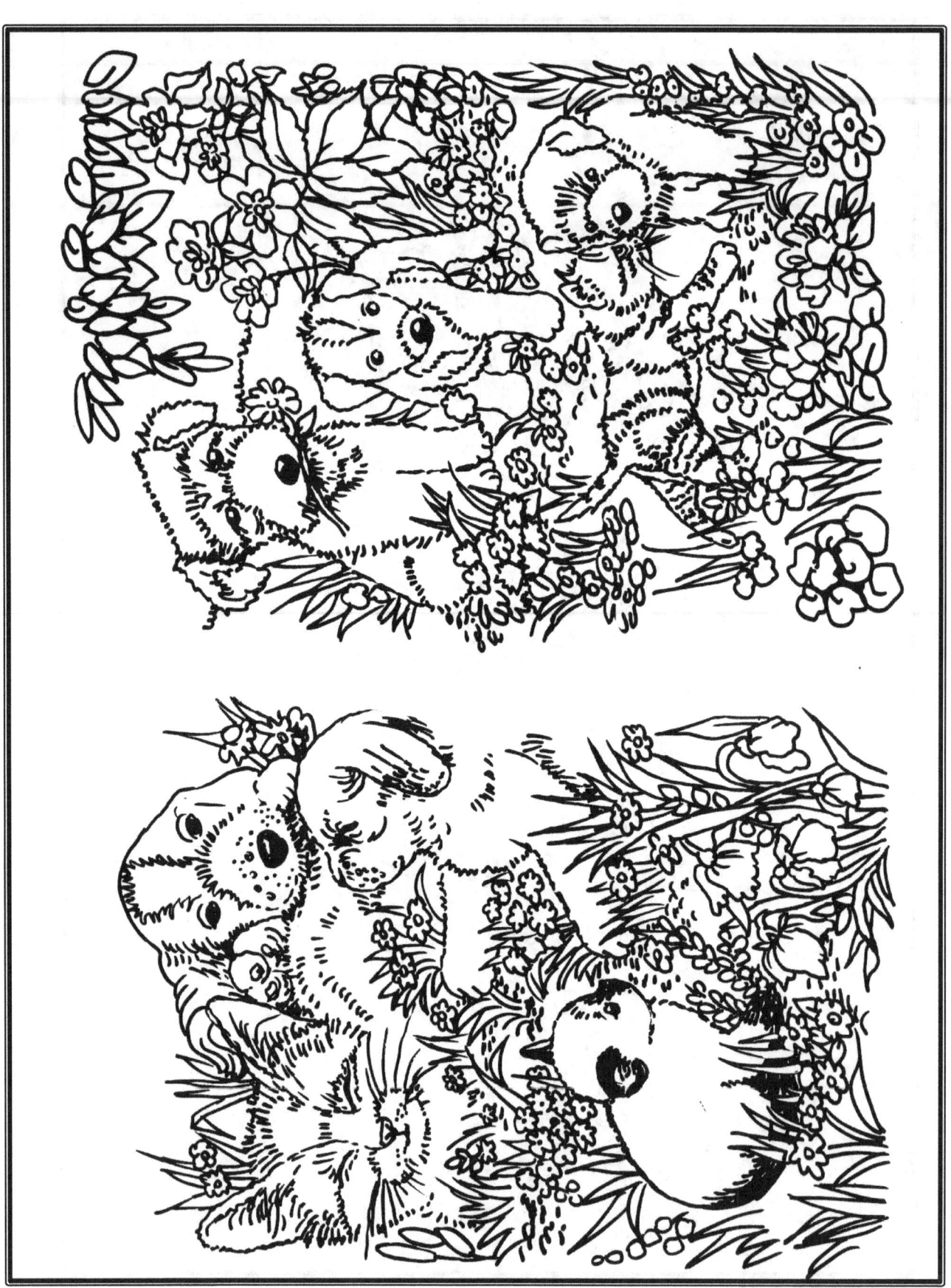

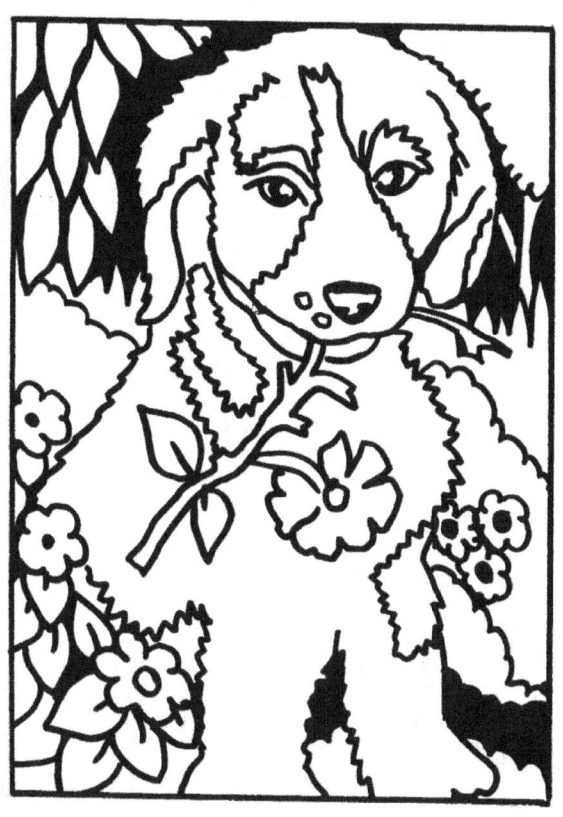
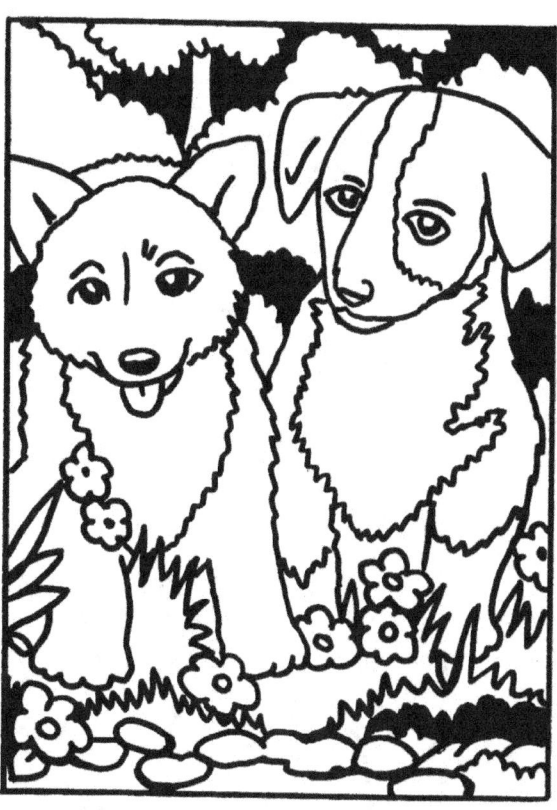
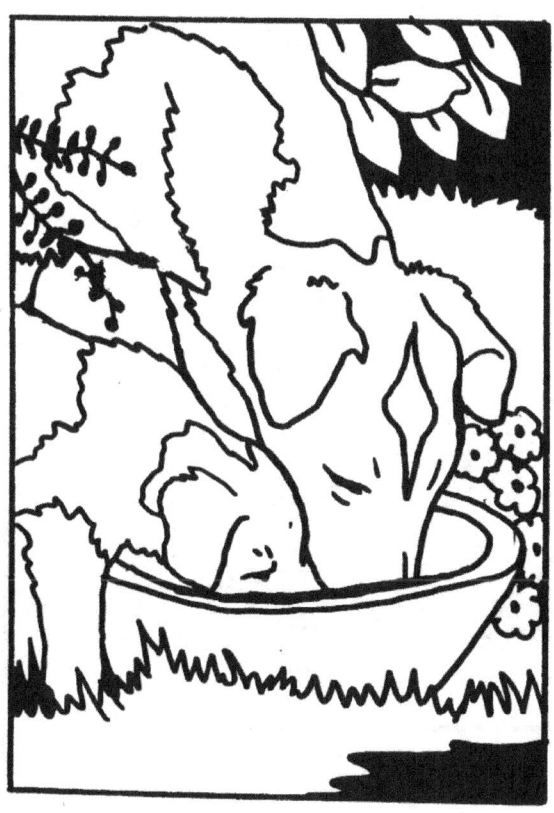
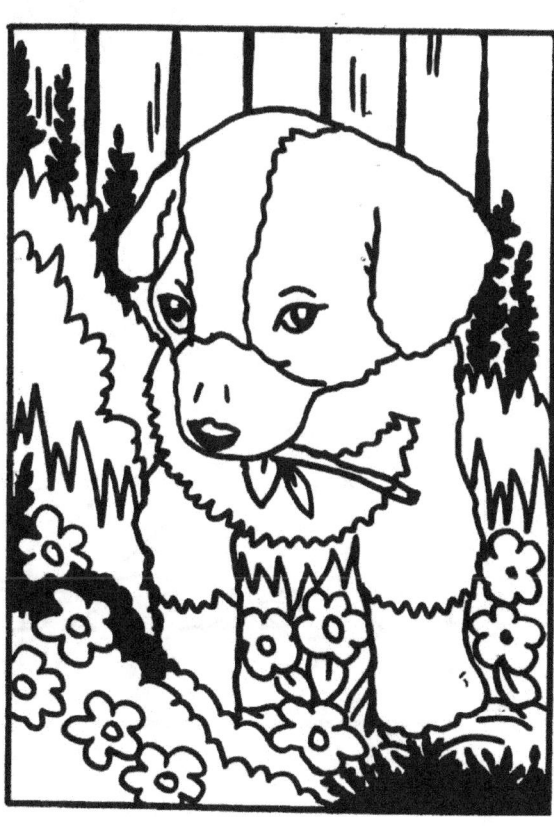

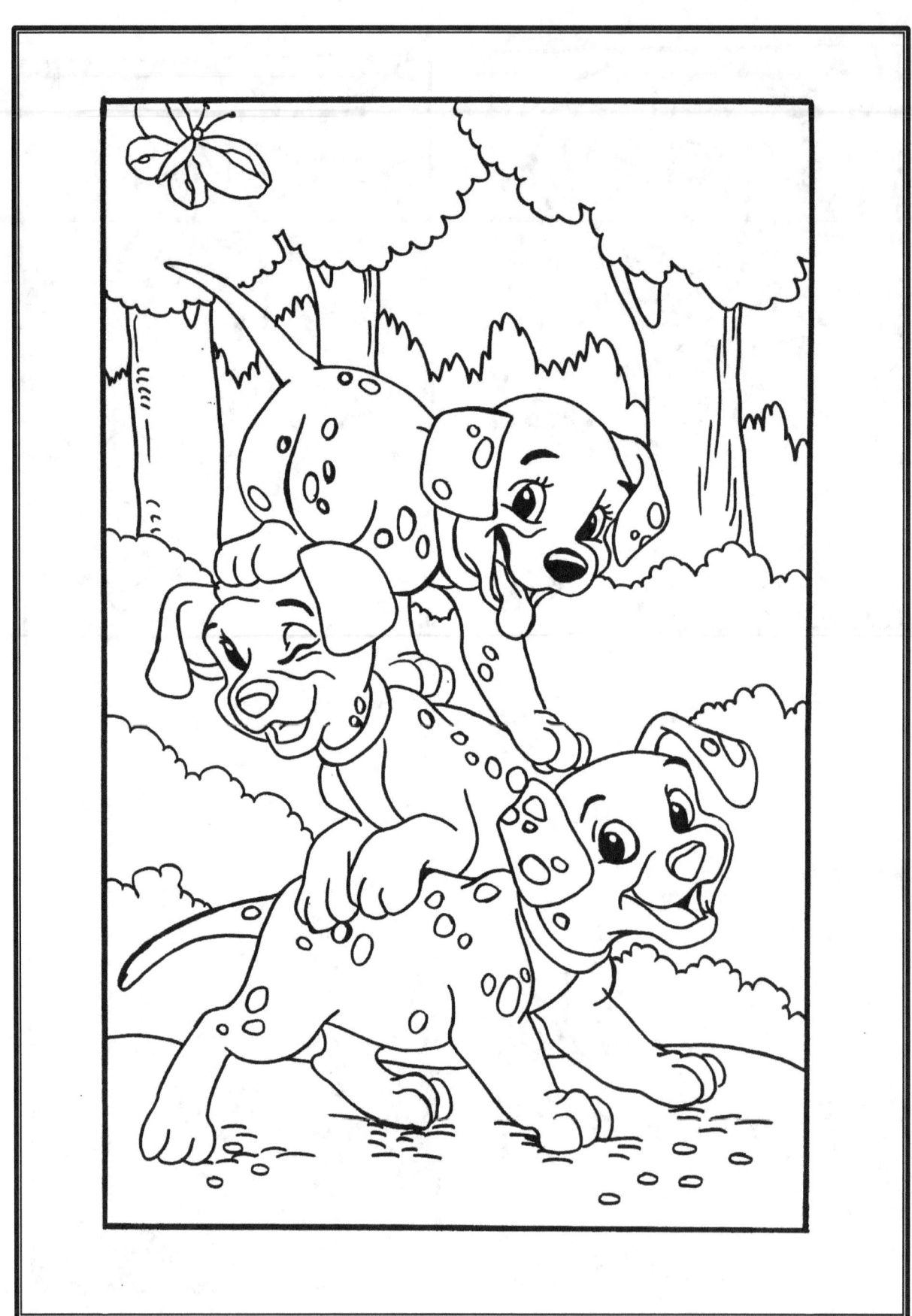

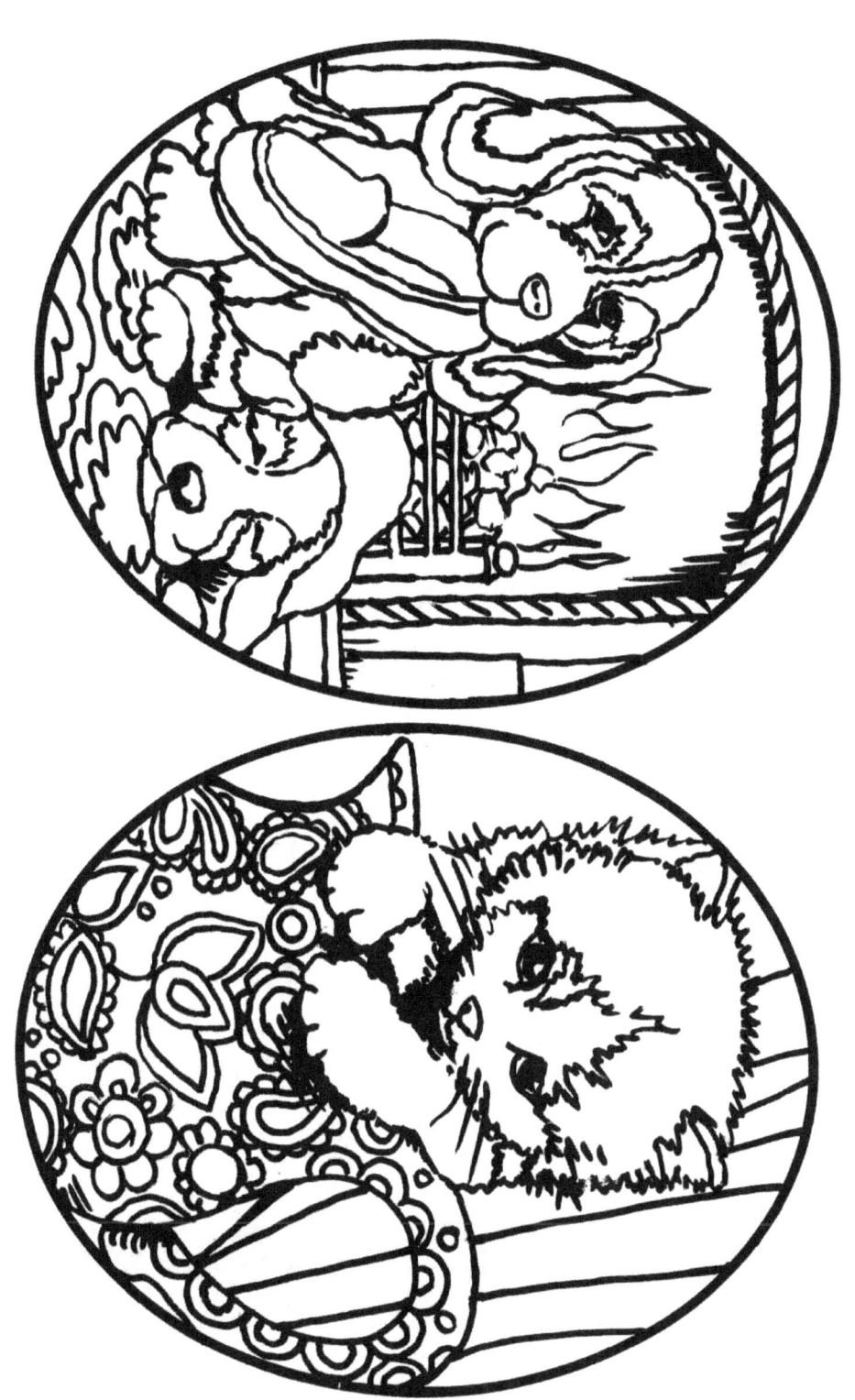